Riddle-icious

by J. Patrick Lewis

illustrated by Debbie Tilley

DRAGONFLY BOOKS™ • Alfred A. Knopf • New York

To Polly, Marie, and Samantha;
Francy, Paula, Linda, and Carol;
and to the memory of Pat
—J. P. L.

For my little buddies Shane, Dylan,
Eric, Ian, Melissa, and Heidi
—Love, Debbie

DRAGONFLY BOOKS™ PUBLISHED BY ALFRED A, KNOPF, INC.

Text copyright © 1996 by J. Patrick Lewis
Illustrations copyright © 1996 by Debbie Tilley

http://www.randomhouse.com/

Library of Congress Cataloging-in-Publication Data
Lewis, J. Patrick.
Riddle-icious / by J. Patrick Lewis ; illustrated by Debbie Tilley.
p.   cm.
1. Riddles, Juvenile. [1. Poetry, American.   2. Riddles.   3. Jokes.]
I. Tilley, Debbie, ill.   II. Title.
PN6371.5.L47   1996
818'.5402—dc20   93-43759

ISBN 0-679-84011-7 (trade) — 0-679-94011-1 (lib. bdg.)
0-679-88545-5 (pbk.)
First Dragonfly Books™ edition: March 1997

Printed in the United States of America
10 9 8 7 6 5 4 3 2 1

Poems that hide
Behind disguises
Tickle you with
Small surprises.
Look inside!
My fondest wish is
You'll find riddles
Riddle-icious!
—J. P. L.

Come right in.
Look around
At all the treasures
That are bound
To make you glad
For a week or two
Until your treasure's
Overdue.

Every fall
this vegeta-ball
welcomes night
by candlelight.

A Pumpkin

If you
eat it
over-
under,
butter
dribbles
down
your
chin.

If you eat it sideways, though, sometimes you might
miss a row.

Corn on the Cob

To folks in Maine
They're red and round,
And you can find them
Underground.

In Idaho
They're brown and big,
But still grow under-
Ground. You dig?

Potatoes

It runs its hands around its face,
It has no legs but runs in place.
Night or day you can depend
Upon it time and time again.

Has two long ears but cannot hear,
Has one big eye but cannot see,
Has no tongue but talks all day.

A Clock

A TV Set

Mr. Silverbright cuts butter.
Mrs. Silverbright pokes peas.
Baby Silverbright scoops soup,
If you please.

A Knife, Fork, and Spoon

This
Sky-
High
Pirate
Steals
Gold
From
The
Sun,
Hides
Moon-
Silver,
Captures
Stars,
One
By
One.

A Cloud

My tricks are easy to remember,
Tie my string around your finger:
Rock-the-Baby-in-the-Cradle,
Walk-the-Doggie down the lane,
Fly me Backward-Round-the-World,
Then Loop-the-Loop me home again.

The tall handsome lady
On Uncle Sam's porch
Stands still as a statue
Holding a torch.

The Statue of Liberty

This ani-mule
Is, as a rule,
Impossible
To push or pull.

A Donkey

Laid back on his pad,
He likes to think,
But having thunk,
He'd rather blink
And having blunk,
Decides to sink,
And having sunk . . .
ka-plink
ka-plunk!

A Frog

I am a helmet
on the ground,
but so afraid of strangers,

I disappear
inside my hat.
The world is full of dangers.

A Turtle

Born in the woods,
Shaped by hand.
Tall in the wind,
Flat on the sand.
Lives on the sea,
Dies on land.

A Sailboat

It sits
on the shore,
silent, alone,
but pick it up
and listen!
This long-wave
radio plays
the same old
Ocean Blues.

SNAP

His back is wide
Enough to ride.
His nose is fun—
A long squirt gun.
His ears, perhaps,
Are giant flaps.
The teeth you see
Are ivory.

An Elephant

Standing under summer skies,
Her back end's good for swatting flies.

If there's nothing else to do,
Her front end's good for making moo.

Front to back and in between,
She's the original cream machine.

A Cow

Twenty-six soldiers,
Who can they be?
One asks, Y?
Another says, G!
Some say, U R A O K!
Twenty-six soldiers,
Z to A.

What's in a song, but not in a tune?
What's in a star, but not in the moon?
What's in the sun, but gone in the night,
Out of range, but still in sight?

It rambles through mountains,
It rumbles through town,
It whistles whenever
   It wants to slow down.

When you are near it,
It hisses and steams,
But once you get *on* it,
   How gentle it seems.

A Train

As I was driving to Van Nuys,
I met a hangman who had three eyes.
Bloodshot the one—it stopped me cold.
The second blinked a shocking gold.
But when the third turned green as grass,
The three-eyed hangman let me pass.

A Traffic Light

The King has three brothers,
The Queen has three sisters,
The Duke has three cousins
(Each one named Jack).

Now how do they know where
Their children are playing?
Each one wears a suit
With a number on back!

I am you
but bigger than you
and longer than you
and darker than you

You are me
but smaller than me
and shorter than me
and scared of me

Your Shadow

After the heavy traffic of rain
The sun gives the green light
To a truck of colors making
A U-turn in the sky.

A Rainbow

Some go in,
Some go out,
Halfway up from your toes.

Some go out,
Some go in,
Halfway down from your nose.

Which tree can hang
    Along a lake,
Whose branches bend
    But will not break,

Whose leaves, sun-summered
    Into bloom,
Can whisk the water
    Like a broom?

Which tree will sigh
    As ripples pass
Across the crystal
    Looking glass,

Then lean beyond
    The shore's long shelf,
Reflecting sadly
    On itself?

A Weeping Willow

Like little red poppies,
They grow in the sun,
One hundred, two hundred,
A thousand and one!
The redder your head,
The farther they spread.

Freckles

I stand in water and I needle the cat. I get spruced up in my angel-hat. Tomorrow morning there will be something for you un-der-neath me.

A Christmas Tree